EXPLORING NATURE AROUND THE YEAR

FALL

Fahey

EXPLORING NATURE AROUND THE YEAR

FALL

DAVID WEBSTER
PICTURES BY BARBARA STEADMAN

JULIAN MESSNER

Text copyright © 1989 by David Webster
Illustrations copyright © 1989 by Barbara Steadman
All rights reserved including the right of reproduction
in whole or in part in any form. Published by Julian
Messner, a division of Silver Burdett Press, Inc.,
Simon & Schuster, Inc. Prentice Hall Bldg.,
Englewood Cliffs, NJ 07632.

JULIAN MESSNER and colophon are trademarks of
Simon & Schuster, Inc.

Design by Malle N. Whitaker

Manufactured in the United States of America.

(Lib. bdg.) 10 9 8 7 6 5 4 3 2 1
(Pbk.)   10 9 8 7 6 5 4 3 2 1

Library of Congress Cataloging-in-Publication Data

Webster, David, 1930–
    Exploring nature around the year : fall / David
    Webster.
        p.   cm.
    Includes index.
    Summary: A collection of activities and projects
exploring nature in the fall.
    1. Autumn—Juvenile literature.   2. Nature
study—Juvenile literature. [1. Autumn. 2. Nature
study.] I. Title.
QH81.W439 1989   508—dc20   89-3262
CIP   AC
ISBN   0-671-65860-3
ISBN   0-671-65985-5 (pbk)

CONTENTS

INTRODUCTION

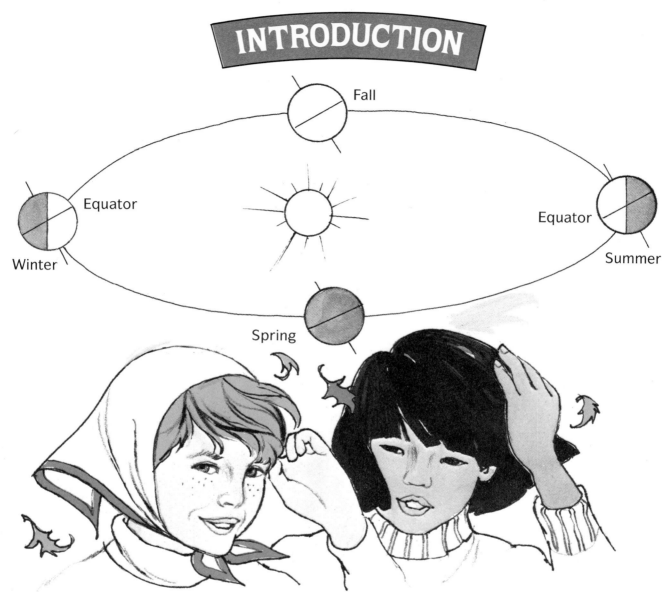

Everyone knows that the year is divided into four seasons: fall, winter, spring, and summer. But how do you know when fall starts? You can look at a calendar: the thirteen weeks of fall begin around September 21 and end about December 21. But there are other ways to tell that fall is starting. You might have to put on warmer clothes, especially in the early morning and the evening, because the air is cooler. You might notice that the mornings are darker as you go to school.

The seasons are caused by the way the earth travels around the sun. In the fall, the sun gives less heat to the earth and the days become shorter. During the summer it stays light until after eight o'clock at night. But by Halloween it may be dark before six o'clock in the evening.

In every season you can see changes in the natural world. The sky and the earth look different in fall from the way they looked in summer. Even the air may feel different—cool and crisp instead of warm and humid.

Animals are busy in the fall as they prepare for cold weather. Squirrels build larger leaf nests and gather plenty of nuts for winter feeding. Many birds migrate by flying south to places where the winter is milder. Bears find secret dens where they can sleep through the winter in hibernation. Many insects lay eggs in the fall; the adult insects die during the winter, but their eggs will hatch in the spring.

8

Plants also change in the fall. The leaves of many trees turn color and silently fall to the ground. Many weeds and other plants turn brown and stop growing. Their seeds drop to the ground, where they remain inactive until aroused by warm spring rains. Some trees scatter their seeds in ripened fruits and nuts.

Every season of the year offers a chance to see exciting changes in the outdoors. In fall, go outside and look for signs of autumn in your back yard, an empty lot, a playground, or a field or forest. Can you discover ways that animals and plants are preparing for winter? Can you see changes that have taken place since the warm summer ended? Even in the supermarket you can see changes, as the fall harvests of fresh apples, ears of corn, and orange pumpkins arrive.

This book can help you enjoy and understand the things that make fall a special time of year.

9

LEAVES

FALLING LEAVES

It is fun to watch leaves fall from trees. Look for a tree that is losing its leaves. Sit down and watch the leaves falling slowly to the ground. Do they drop straight down or wobble back and forth? What happens when the wind blows?

Watch one leaf and count how long it takes to reach the ground. Why do you think leaves fall at different speeds? Do big leaves fall faster than smaller ones?

As the flat leaf blade falls, it is slowed down by the air. A leaf is like a parachute.

You can see what air does by dropping two pieces of paper. First, crumple up one piece of paper into a tight wad. Then drop the wad and the unfolded paper at the same time. Which hits the floor first? Why does the air slow down the unfolded paper? Flat paper must push aside more air than a crumpled piece of paper does.

10

PARACHUTE

It is easy to make a little parachute. You will need:

1. A piece of thin cloth about 1 foot square, such as a handkerchief or bandana

2. Some thin string

3. A weight, such as a pebble or a large nut

Tie a piece of string, about a foot long, to each corner of the cloth. Tie the bottom of each string to the weight. Tape or a rubber band will help you attach the strings to the weight.

Now you are ready to launch your parachute. Fold the cloth and wrap the strings loosely around it with the weight on the outside. Throw the parachute as high as you can into the air. If the string does not unwrap, try it again.

Does your parachute fall as slowly as a leaf?

Parachutes are worn by skydivers who jump from airplanes. Parachutes also are needed to slow down the space shuttle when it returns from space to earth.

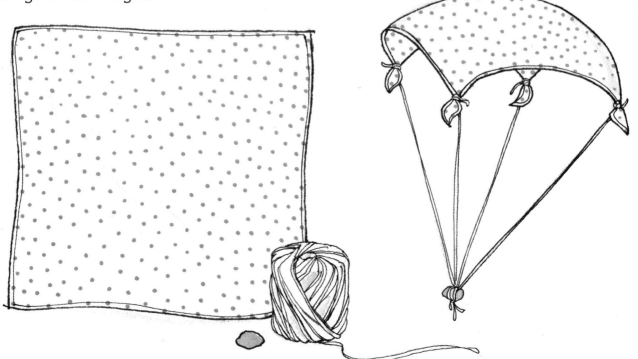

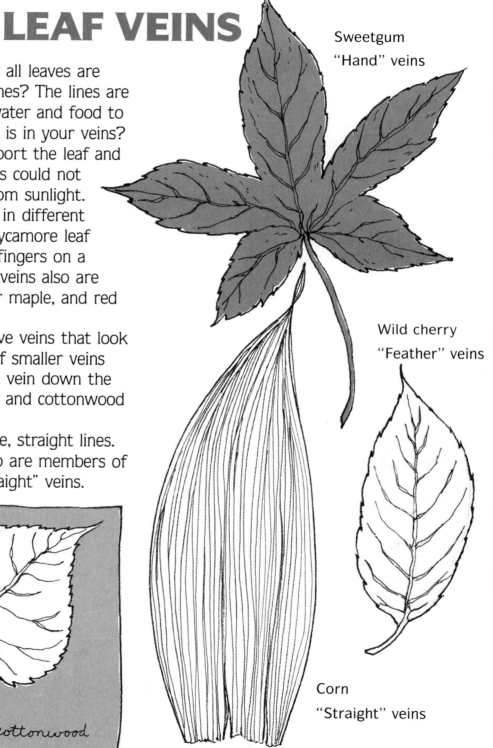

LEAF VEINS

Sweetgum
"Hand" veins

Have you noticed that all leaves are covered by lots of lines? The lines are called veins. Veins carry water and food to all parts of the leaf. What is in your veins?

The veins also help support the leaf and make it stiff. Floppy leaves could not collect as much energy from sunlight.

Leaf veins are arranged in different patterns. The veins of a sycamore leaf might remind you of the fingers on a hand. Leaves with "hand" veins also are found on sweetgum, silver maple, and red maple trees.

Other kinds of trees have veins that look like a feather. Hundreds of smaller veins branch out from the main vein down the center. Beech, wild cherry, and cottonwood trees have "feather" veins.

Grass veins look like fine, straight lines. Corn, cattails, and bamboo are members of the grass family with "straight" veins.

Wild cherry
"Feather" veins

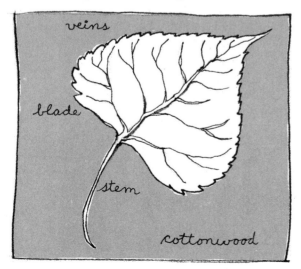

veins

blade

stem

cottonwood

Corn
"Straight" veins

12

LEAF RUBBINGS

You can copy leaf veins by making a rubbing. Here is how to do it:

1. Place a leaf upside down on a work table or desk.

2. Cover the leaf with a sheet of white paper.

3. Rub a crayon back and forth over the leaf until you have covered the whole leaf.

Try to make rubbings to show all three kinds of veins.

LEAF BOOK

You can probably find leaves in all sizes and shapes. Collect about twelve leaves from different trees and bushes. Some colorful red or yellow leaves will make your collection more interesting.

Neatly mount the leaves on sheets of paper with transparent tape. Put three or four leaves on each piece of paper.

Try to label each leaf with its proper name. The shape of a leaf can help tell you the name of the tree it came from. Aspen trees have roundish leaves, and birch leaves are triangular. The points around

the edge of an elm leaf are called teeth. Ask someone to help you identify unknown leaves with a tree guide from the library.

Staple your pages together to make a leaf book. You can include rubbings of leaf veins. Draw pictures of colored leaves to make a cover.

When your book is done, place it under some heavy books for several weeks. The leaves will curl up and lose their shape if they are not pressed flat as they dry out.

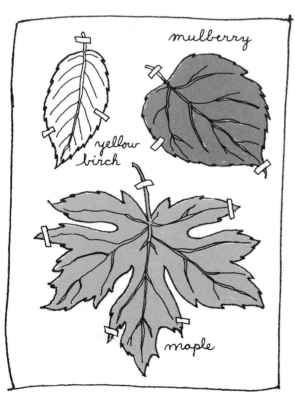

14

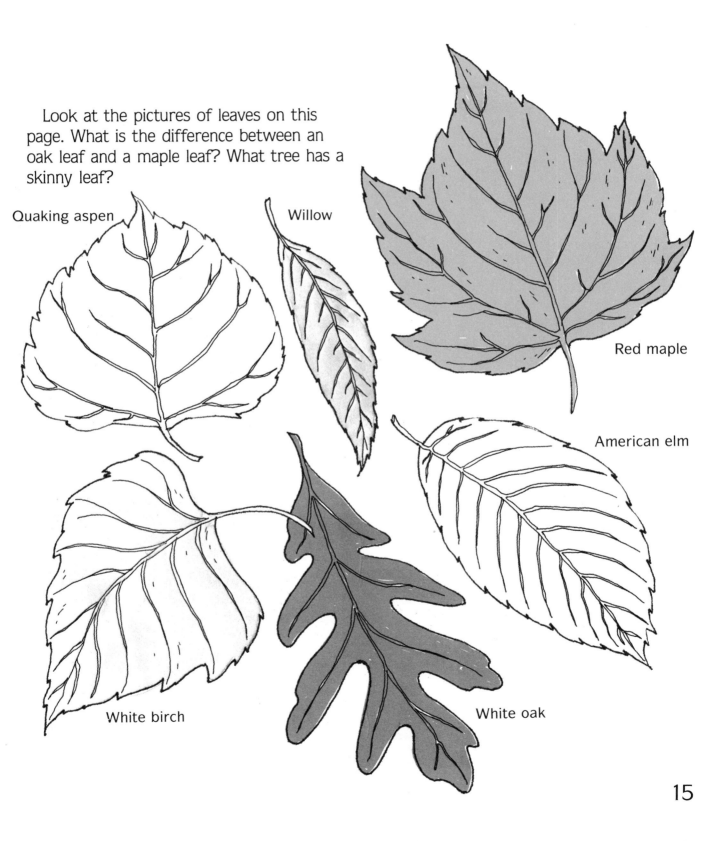

Look at the pictures of leaves on this page. What is the difference between an oak leaf and a maple leaf? What tree has a skinny leaf?

Quaking aspen

Willow

Red maple

American elm

White birch

White oak

15

LEAF MONSTER

Here's how to make a leaf monster. First, collect colorful leaves of different shapes. Then paste them to a piece of paper in the shape of a monster.

Find a nice large leaf for the body of your monster and a smaller one for the head. Skinny leaves are good to use for the arms and legs. Small, pointed leaves make scary fingers. It is all right to cut some leaves with scissors to make better shapes. For a face, glue on seeds or tiny leaves.

When your monster is finished, press it for several weeks between a few sheets of newspaper. Put some heavy books on top of the newspaper to keep it flat.

16

EVERGREEN NEEDLES

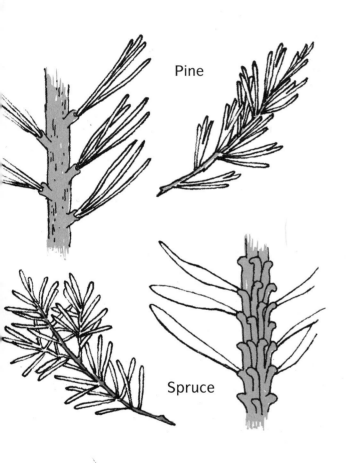

Pine

Spruce

Evergreen trees have needle-like leaves instead of the larger, flat leaves of other trees. Pine, spruce, fir, cedar, and hemlock are some common evergreen trees.

Even though these trees are always green, they do drop needles in the fall. But they only drop some of their needles.

Find an evergreen tree so you can watch its needles during the fall. The needles that drop off are the brown ones toward the inside of the branch. Look on the ground under the tree. Have lots of dead needles fallen off yet? You can make a needle collection to add to your leaf collection.

Evergreen trees have needles of different sizes and shapes. Pines have long, flexible needles. The needles of spruce are four-sided and grow close together. The balsam fir, which is often used as a Christmas tree, has a white line on the underside of its flat needle. Hemlocks have two rows of short, flat needles with tiny stalks.

Balsam

Hemlock

17

INSIDE AN APPLE

Apples are harvested in the fall. Do you know what an apple looks like inside? Guess which of the drawings on this page are apples.

For a look inside, get two apples. Have an adult help you cut them in half with a kitchen knife. Cut one the long way from top to bottom, and cut the other in half crosswise.

Compare the insides of the apples with the drawings. Do you see any differences in their shapes?

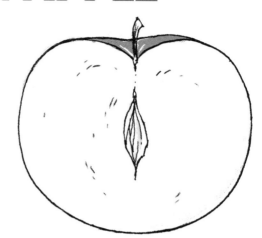

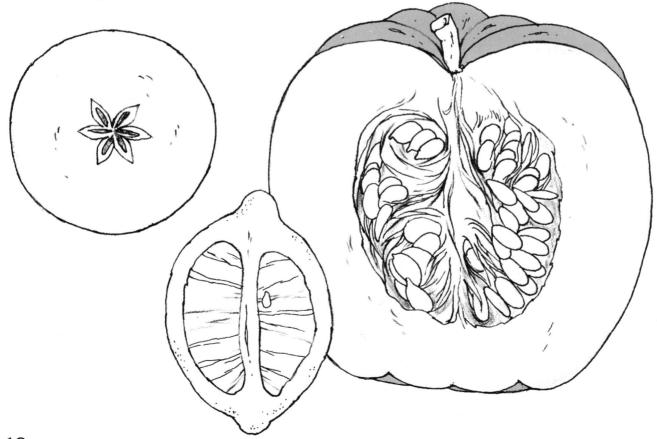

18

The part of the apple you eat is called pulp. The core is in the center and holds the seeds. Dig out all the seeds from the core of one apple. How many did you find?

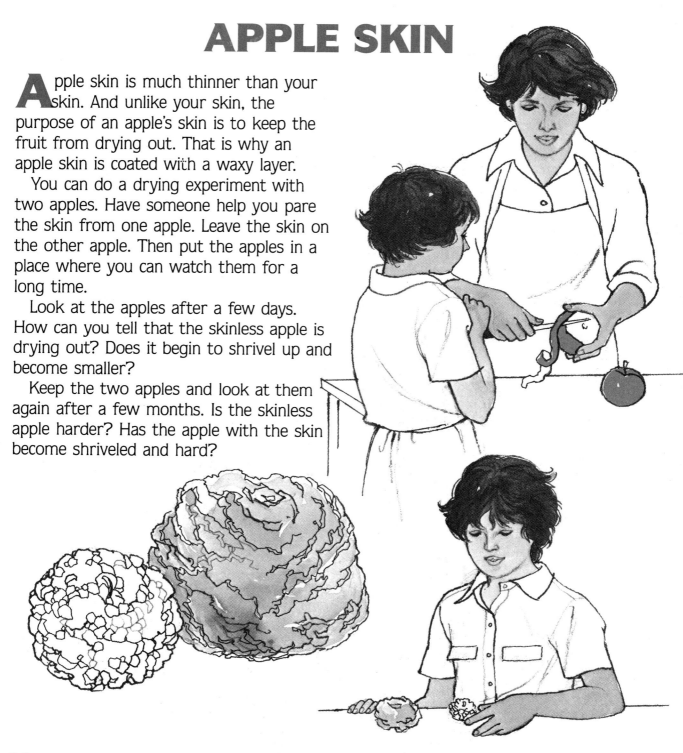

APPLE SKIN

Apple skin is much thinner than your skin. And unlike your skin, the purpose of an apple's skin is to keep the fruit from drying out. That is why an apple skin is coated with a waxy layer.

You can do a drying experiment with two apples. Have someone help you pare the skin from one apple. Leave the skin on the other apple. Then put the apples in a place where you can watch them for a long time.

Look at the apples after a few days. How can you tell that the skinless apple is drying out? Does it begin to shrivel up and become smaller?

Keep the two apples and look at them again after a few months. Is the skinless apple harder? Has the apple with the skin become shriveled and hard?

20

APPLE VARIETIES

Red Delicious

McIntosh

Granny Smith

Golden Delicious

Variety	Skin Color	Shape	Pulp Color	Smell
McIntosh	Red and Green	Round	Off white	Sweet
Red Delicious	Shiny Red	Oblong	Pale Yellow	Faint
Golden Delicious	Yellow Black Dots	Oblong	Pale Yellow	None
Granny Smith	Green	Round	Pale Yellow	Faint

There are many different kinds, or varieties, of apples. McIntosh, Red Delicious, Golden Delicious, and Granny Smith are among the most popular varieties. Ask an adult to buy you three or four different kinds of apples.

Probably the first thing you will notice about the apples is their color differences. Red Delicious apples are all red, and McIntosh are red with patches of green. Other kinds of apples never are red;

Golden Delicious are yellow and Granny Smith are green.

What do you notice about the apples' shapes? Which varieties are the roundest? Do any have bumps on the bottom?

Have someone help you cut the apples in half. Is the pulp of all the apples the same color?

You can make a chart to compare apple varieties. Find as many differences as you can.

21

TASTE TESTS

Do all apples taste the same? You can find out by making a taste test.

Ask an adult to cut different kinds of apples into slices. Keep the slices of each variety together. Eat one slice of each. Which do you like best? Are any of the apples unsweet? Are they crisp or soft? Are some apples juicier than others?

Let other people taste the apples, too. Keep track of their likes and dislikes on a score card. Which apple is most popular?

The varieties of apples that are less popular for eating may be better in other ways. They might be good for making apple pie or applesauce.

Food companies hire people to taste new foods. The tasters help the company decide which foods are best to sell. They might sample different kinds of soda or soup or cookies. Now you are an apple taster.

22

CIDER AND APPLE JUICE

In Colonial days, cider was the most popular drink. It was made in the fall from the juice of crushed apples.

Fresh apple cider will only stay sweet for about a week. Then it slowly ferments and turns "hard" as the apple sugar changes into alcohol. The fermentation process is caused by tiny plants called yeast. Canned apple juice is cider that has been cooked to kill the yeast.

If you have some cider, put some in a glass. Let it stand outside the refrigerator for a week or so. In a few days you should notice that small gas bubbles have formed on the inside of the glass. The bubbles are carbon dioxide gas which is given off by the growing yeast cells.

Taste a little of the fermenting cider. The bitter taste comes from the alcohol.

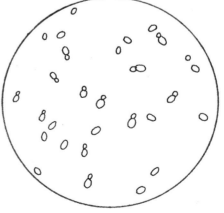

Yeast cells

23

PUMPKIN SEEDS

Pumpkins have more seeds than apples do. How many seeds do you think are inside a pumpkin? 100? More than 200?

To find out, you will need a pumpkin. Have a grownup help you cut it in half with a large kitchen knife. Scoop out the seeds and slimy strings from each half, and count the seeds. How many are there?

Look at three or four seeds. Are they all exactly the same size and shape? With your fingernail, split open one seed and see what is inside. The hard outside of a seed is called the seed coat. The softer part inside contains the embryo, which sprouts when the seed is planted.

24

ROTTEN PUMPKINS

Have you ever seen a rotten pumpkin? Maybe your jack-o-lantern was left outside after Halloween and started to rot.

Here is how to do a rotting experiment with two pumpkin halves. Put one pumpkin half outside where it will not be disturbed. Keep the other half in your room on a newspaper.

Look at the pumpkins again in a week. Has the outside pumpkin begun to rot?

Can you see any mold growing on the inside pumpkin?

Try to remember to look at the pumpkins every week. How can you tell that the inside pumpkin is drying up? What will the pumpkins look like after several months?

Rotting is caused by tiny plants called bacteria and molds. Bacteria need water to live. Why does a pumpkin stop rotting when it dries out?

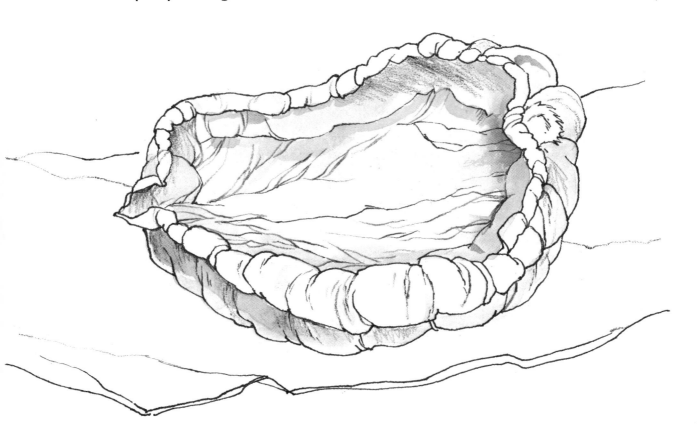

25

SEED COLLECTIONS

Seeds begin inside flowers. After the flowers die, the seeds continue to grow. Many seeds are not ripe until late summer and fall.

You should be able to gather plenty of seeds to make a nice collection and to use for an art project. Get ten or twelve plastic sandwich bags for carrying the seeds.

A field is a good place to begin your seed hunt. Look for bunches of seeds clinging to dead flower stalks. Shake or pull off the seeds into one of the plastic bags. Use a different bag for each kind of seed.

Berries are seeds, too. Look for clusters of berries on bushes and in low tree branches. Bright, colorful berries may look good enough to eat, but do not eat any. Some kinds of berries are poisonous!

26

Mount your seeds on a piece of cardboard or poster paper. Pick a few samples of each kind and attach them with tape or glue. Label any seeds you can identify.

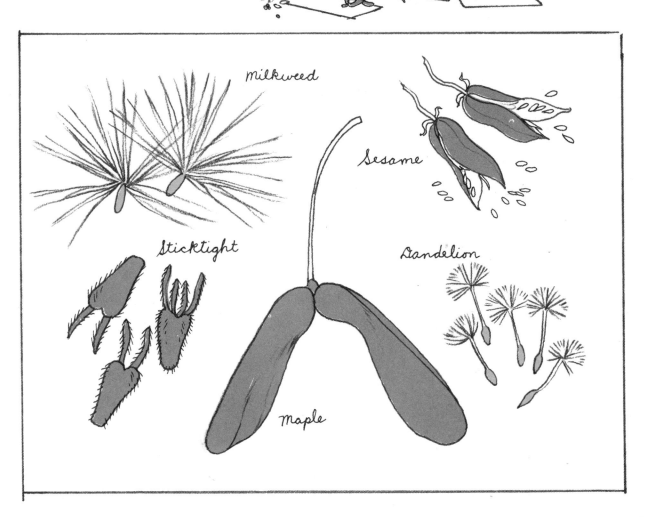

milkweed

Sesame

Sticktight

Dandelion

Maple

TREE SEEDS

Nuts are larger seeds from trees. Maybe you can find some acorns, walnuts, horse chestnuts, or beechnuts. Most nuts are covered with a tough outer shell that splits open when the nut is ripe. An acorn's shell is the little cup that holds it to the oak branch.

The softer part of a nut, inside the inner shell, is called the nutmeat. Ask someone to help you cut open an acorn. Inside you might find a little worm eating the nutmeat.

Squirrels, chipmunks, and mice are fond of nuts. These animals need strong front teeth to gnaw through hard nutshells. Place some nuts outside to see if they are eaten. Count the nuts first so you will know if any disappear.

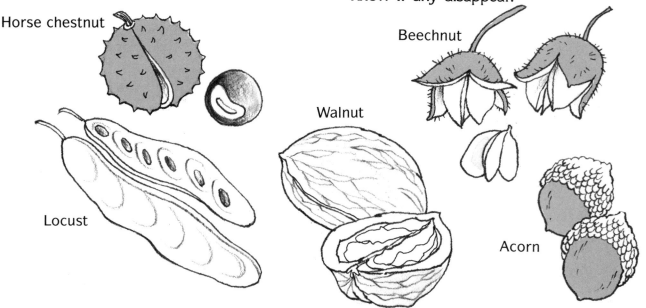

Horse chestnut

Beechnut

Walnut

Locust

Acorn

28

People like to eat nuts, too. Look for walnuts, almonds, pecans, and peanuts in the supermarket. Can you find out how peanuts are different from other nuts?

Pine tree seeds come from pine cones. Look for cones that are still green and unopened. When kept in your warm house, the cone scales will dry out and open with a snap to uncover the seeds inside. Red squirrels often tear apart pine cones in order to eat the seeds.

Locust and catalpa trees have seeds inside long seed pods. See if you can find a tree with pods.

Of course, nuts can grow into new trees. Plant some nuts in a little tree garden outside. Remember to look next spring to see if any have sprouted. Perhaps your trees will grow to be bigger than you are.

29

BIRD SEED

The birds would like to eat any extra seeds you have.

You can stick a lot of seeds together with some peanut butter. Put three or four teaspoons of peanut butter on a plate and mix in the seeds with your fingers. Messy!

Now get a paper cup and cut off the top half. Push several thumb tacks through the bottom to attach the cup to a tree or post outside your house. Put the cup in a place where you can see it from inside.

Push the peanut butter and seed mixture into the cup. Stick in a short pencil to make a perch for the birds to land on.

Check the feeder in a few days to see if any seed is being eaten. It may take a while for the birds to find their treat.

Many kinds of birds, such as sparrows, finches, and wrens, eat only seeds. It must take a lot of time to gather enough small seeds to make a meal.

30

ANIMALS PREPARE FOR WINTER

COCOON HUNT

Cooler nights and shorter days signal animals that winter is coming. Many caterpillars spin cocoons in the fall. During the winter, inside the cocoon, the caterpillar turns into a moth. When the weather warms up in the spring, the moth hatches and flies away.

A cocoon looks like a small, fuzzy egg. The best place to search for them is in a field after the weeds die. Look for fuzzy bags hanging from plant stalks. Break off the plant stem with the cocoon still attached.

Keep your cocoon inside a jar in the refrigerator. The moth will not hatch unless it is cold for many months. In the spring, when the weather gets warm, take the cocoon out of the refrigerator. Leave it inside the jar. Maybe you will be lucky and see a moth hatch.

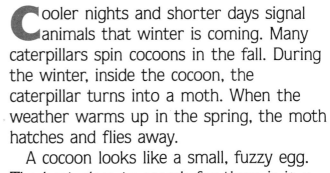

MIGRATING BIRDS

Bobolink

Sparrow

Baltimore oriole

Swallow

Birds and mammals have different ways of surviving the winter. A few animals hibernate, or go into a deep sleep during the cold months. Others grow a heavier coat of fur and remain active regardless of the weather. Some animals migrate to warmer places.

No matter where you live, you should be able to notice the migration of some birds. Ask an adult to take you on a few nature walks during the fall so you can watch the birds.

If you live in the north, you might have seen robins, swallows, sparrows, red-winged blackbirds, Baltimore orioles, bobolinks, ducks, or geese during the summer. All of these birds migrate. What birds disappear from your area during the fall?

If you live in the south, you may notice that new birds appear in the fall. Have you seen any strangers? Some new birds might stay only for a few days and then continue their flight south. Other kinds might be with you all winter.

BIRD NESTS

The best time to find bird nests is in the fall after the birds have migrated. It is all right to take any nests you discover. Birds use their nests only in the spring when the babies hatch, and they make new nests every year.

Look for nests in bushes and low tree branches. If you find a nest, try to figure out what materials the birds used to make it. Some birds use twigs and grass, while others use shredded bark or moss or horse hair. Robin and grackle nests have a heavy crust of mud.

Look inside the nest for tiny feathers, broken egg shells, and the remains of food.

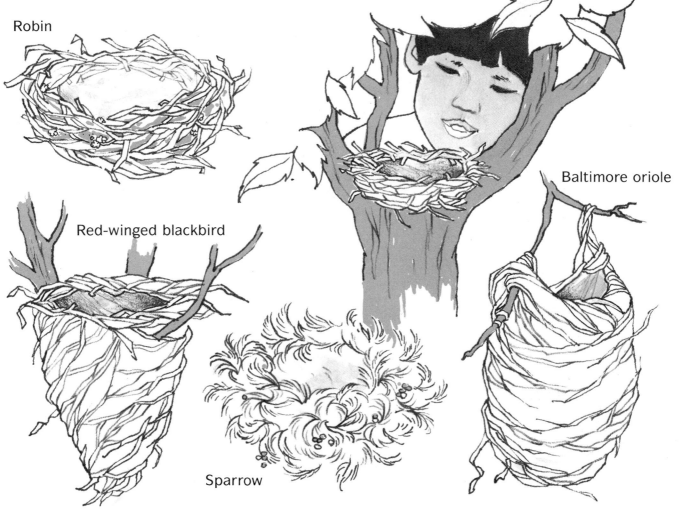

Robin

Baltimore oriole

Red-winged blackbird

Sparrow

SOIL

WHAT IS SOIL?

Most people call it dirt, but scientists call it soil. What is in soil? To find out, you will have to look at it very carefully.

Dig up a cup of soil from outside. Spread out the soil on a sheet of newspaper and pick through it with your fingers. Don't be afraid to get your hands dirty. A magnifying glass will help you see smaller things.

Get a piece of white paper and draw ten small circles on it. Put each kind of thing you find in the soil in a different circle.

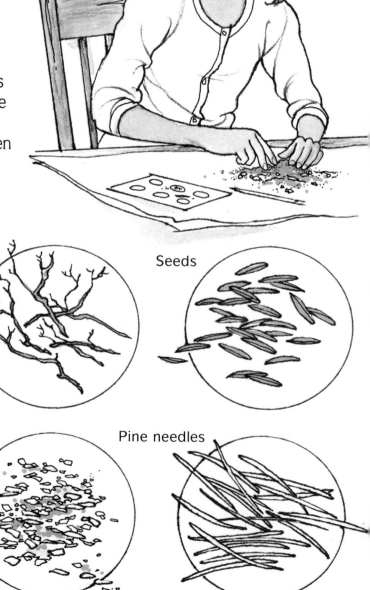

Pebbles

Twigs

Seeds

Leaves

Mica

Pine needles

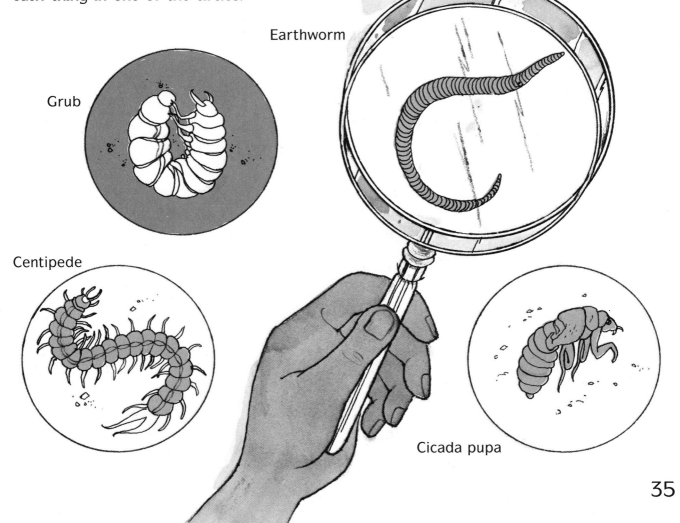

Are there any pebbles in your soil? Some soil has lots of small rocks and other soil has none. Look for sand, which is very small pieces of rock. White sand is probably quartz; shiny flakes are mica. The smallest particles in soil are silt and clay.

Soil often contains parts of plants. Can you find any roots, rotten leaves, seeds, twigs, or pine needles? Put a sample of each thing in one of the circles.

If you are lucky, you might find a live animal in the soil. Ants, beetles, centipedes, earthworms, and grubs live in soil. Grubs look like fat, white bugs. Grubs spend the winter protected by the soil and turn into insects in the spring.

Most soils also contain some water. Has the newspaper under the soil pile become moist?

Earthworm

Grub

Centipede

Cicada pupa

35

SOIL LAYERS

There is an easy way to separate soil particles. All you need is a tall jar with a screw cap. Put soil into the jar until it is about one-third full. Add water, but leave a one-inch air space at the top. Now put on the cap and shake hard to mix the water and soil. Put the jar down and watch the particles settle from the muddy water.

Can you see different layers? The heaviest pebbles will be on the bottom, with sand next, and silt on top. Take off the cap. What is floating on the surface of the water?

The smallest particles, clay, take longer to settle. The cloudy water should clear up in a day or two. When this happens, look for a very thin layer of clay on top of the silt.

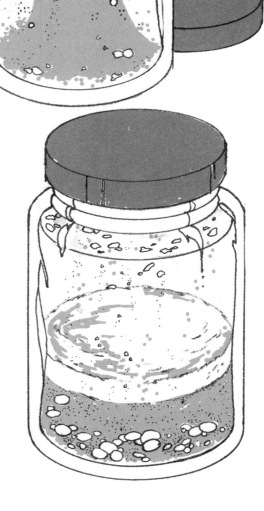

36

THE MOON

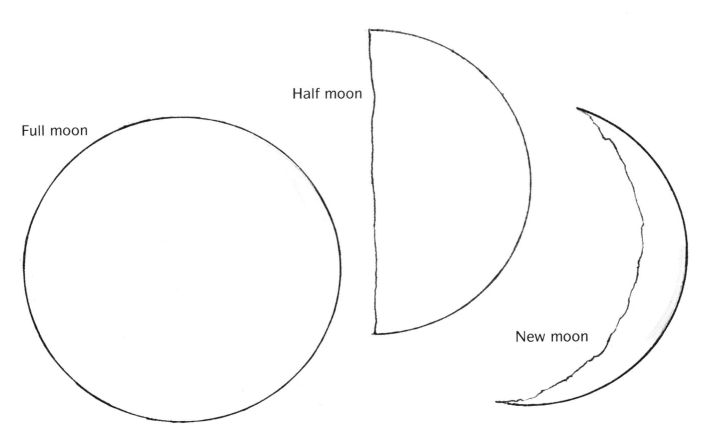

Half moon

Full moon

New moon

The moon is not a star. Unlike a star, the moon is not hot; moonlight is reflected sunlight.

In the fall, a full moon is known as the "harvest moon." A harvest moon seems to be unusually large and yellowish.

Go outside and look for the moon every evening before you go to bed. Can you see the moon on every clear night? Is the moon always in the same place in the sky?

How does the moon change shape? Can you ever see the moon during the day?

Try to use a pair of binoculars to look at the moon. You should be able to see its craters.

The moon's orbit is around the earth. It takes only about four weeks for the moon to orbit the earth. The ancient Romans divided the year into months based on the moon's orbit time.

STAR PATTERNS

Big Dipper

Cassiopeia's Chair

Long ago, people noticed that the stars were arranged in special shapes. Today we call these star patterns constellations.

To see constellations, you must wait until it is completely dark, at least one hour after sunset. The best place for looking is in a large field away from trees and house lights. On a clear night you can see more than 3,000 stars.

One of the easiest constellations to find is the Big Dipper. You should be able to see it in the northern sky. How many stars are in the Big Dipper? Does it look like a big ladle or water dipper?

Cassiopeia's Chair is another constellation you can see toward the north. The five stars in the chair may look more like a big "M" or "W."

38

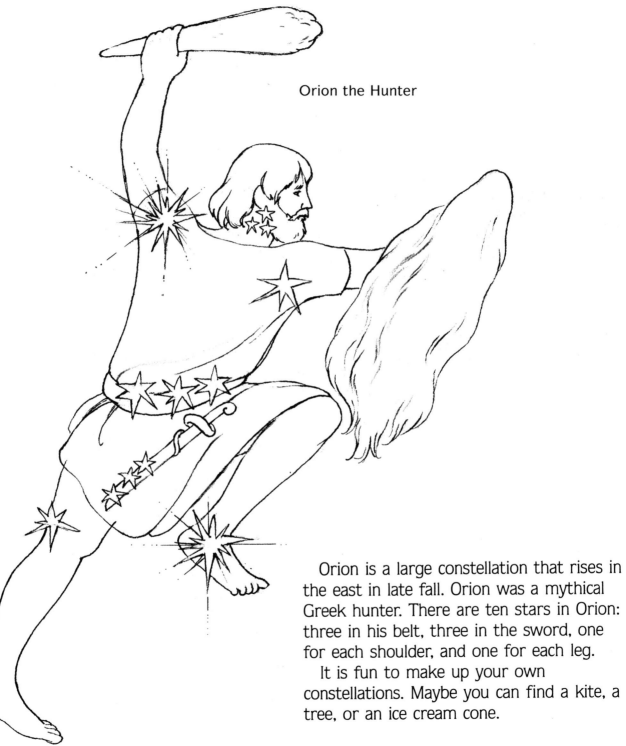

Orion the Hunter

Orion is a large constellation that rises in the east in late fall. Orion was a mythical Greek hunter. There are ten stars in Orion: three in his belt, three in the sword, one for each shoulder, and one for each leg.

It is fun to make up your own constellations. Maybe you can find a kite, a tree, or an ice cream cone.

39

MEASURING THE SUN'S HEAT

The sun heats the earth during the day. At night, the air cools off slowly. What time of day is usually the warmest? You can find out by measuring the outside air temperature with a thermometer.

Do you have an outside thermometer in a window of your house? If not, ask if you can buy one from a hardware store.

Make your measurements at different times on a sunny day. You will need to record the times and temperatures on a piece of paper.

Some people think it is warmest about noon. What time of day did you find was the warmest? Take temperatures on other days to see if the warmest time changes.

DATE	November 12				
WEATHER	Sunny				
TIME	8 A.M.	10 A.M.	12 A.M.	2 P.M.	4 P.M.
TEMPERATURE	36°F	47°F	55°F	57°F	49°F
DATE	November 15				
WEATHER	Sunny				
TEMPERATURE	40°F	49°F	58°F	56°F	42°F
DATE	November 16				

40

MEASURING YOUR SHADOW

Did you know that your shadow is not always the same length? It changes during the day and also at different times of the year.

Ask someone to measure your shadow at three different times during the day. Do it early in the morning, exactly at noon, and again in the late afternoon. You should be standing in the same level place each time. Write down the measurements so you won't forget them. Is your shadow longer when the sun is higher in the sky or lower? When during the day is the sun at its highest point?

Wait for several months and measure your shadow again at noon. Has its length changed? Is the noontime sun higher or lower?

During the winter the sun never gets as high as it does during the summer. This is why the days are shorter in the winter.

41

TURKEY BONES

Before you throw away the remains of your Thanksgiving turkey, clean the bones by cooking them in boiling water in a large pot. Ask an adult to help you. Simmer the bones for several hours until the meat is soft enough to fall off. After cooling, clean each bone by scrubbing it in the sink under running warm water. Lay out the bones on a newspaper to dry.

Try to lay out the bones in the shape of a turkey skeleton. The long bones are from the wings and legs. The knob on the thighbone fits into the socket of the hipbone. The smaller bones from the neck could be held together by stringing them on a piece of thin wire. If you want to save the skeleton, glue the bones to a piece of cardboard.

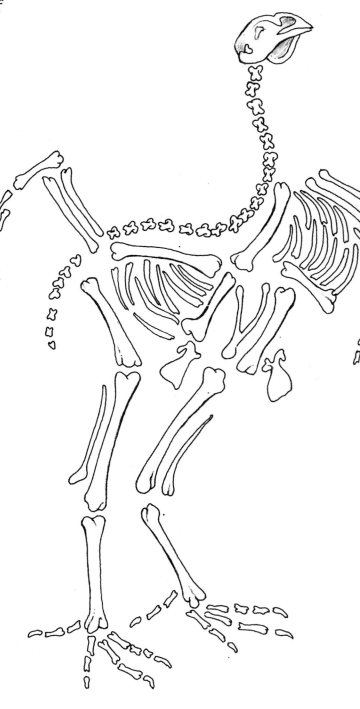

FISH SKELETON

If your family is having fish for dinner, you can preserve a fish skeleton. You need a whole fish, such as a mackerel, ocean perch, herring, or snapper.

Ask an adult to help. When the fish is cooked, the flesh can be cut from the backbone. Clean the skeleton and tail under running water.

The backbone is made up of a chain of small bones called vertebrae. Count how many bones are in the fish's backbone. Are there more than twenty? Bend the backbone from side to side the way a fish does when it swims. Notice the movable joints between the vertebrae.

Most large animals have a backbone. All mammals, birds, reptiles, amphibians, and fish have backbones. The largest animal without a backbone is the giant squid.

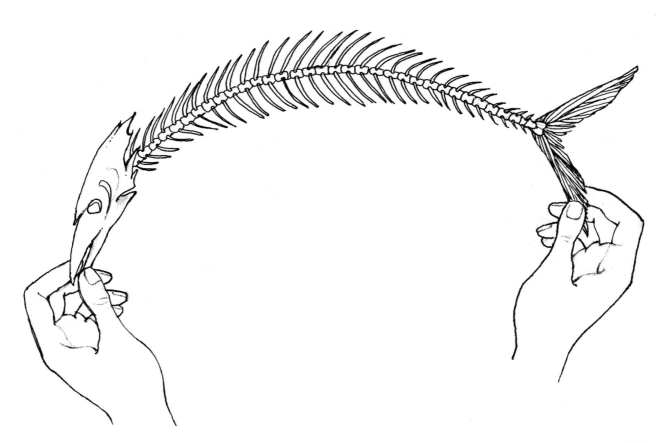

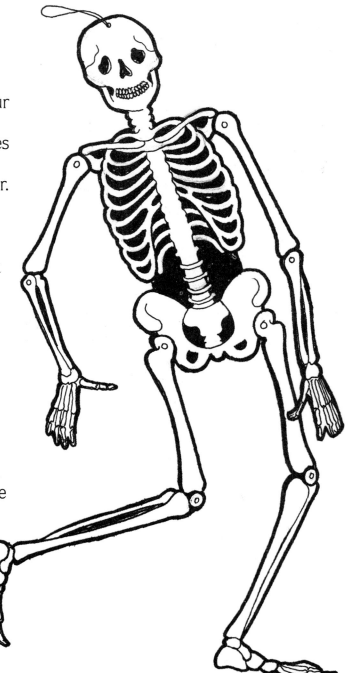

YOUR SKELETON

Halloween is the time for scary skeletons. You have a skeleton of your own hidden under your skin.

You can learn a lot about your skeleton just by looking and feeling. Start with your hand. How many bones do you have in each finger? Can you count fourteen bones in four fingers and a thumb?

Rub the back of your hand with a finger. Can you feel the bones that attach the fingers to the wrist?

Your lower arm has two long bones. Hold your wrist and twist your hand back and forth. Can you feel the two bones moving?

Your jaw also has two bones. Feel the little dent where they are joined together at the chin. Are there bones in your nose and ears?

Your neck and backbone are made of many smaller bones, or vertebrae, connected in a long chain. The bones have bumps that you can feel behind your neck.

The round bone on the knee is called the kneecap. While your leg is limp, wobble your kneecap from side to side with your fingers.

44

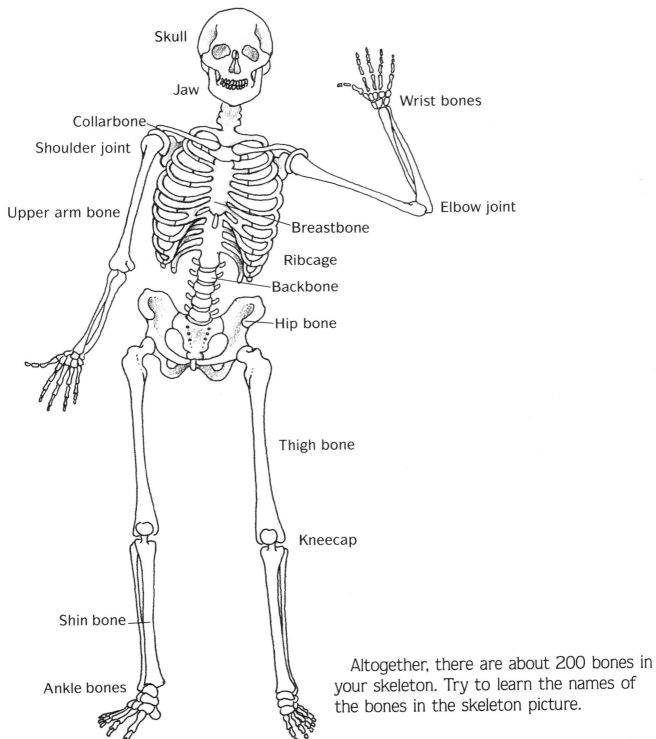

Skull

Jaw

Collarbone

Shoulder joint

Upper arm bone

Wrist bones

Elbow joint

Breastbone

Ribcage

Backbone

Hip bone

Thigh bone

Kneecap

Shin bone

Ankle bones

Altogether, there are about 200 bones in your skeleton. Try to learn the names of the bones in the skeleton picture.

45

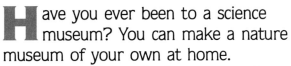

A NATURE MUSEUM

Have you ever been to a science museum? You can make a nature museum of your own at home.

You will need a display area, such as a bookshelf or table, on which to arrange things you find. You could have a seed collection, a bird nest, soil samples, a dried apple, a leaf rubbing, and turkey bones. Make signs to tell about the nature displays.

Your friends might enjoy seeing your nature museum. Then they will know what you've learned outdoors in the fall. Keep your displays and add to them in other seasons of the year.

46

INDEX

ABOUT THE AUTHOR & ARTIST

David Webster teaches elementary science at two schools in Massachusetts. He was a staff member of the elementary science study of the Education Development Center. Mr. Webster has written twelve science books, including *Frog and Toad Watching* and *How to Do a Science Project*. The author lives in Lincoln, Massachusetts, and spends summers on Bailey Island in Maine.

Barbara Steadman studied at the Museum School of Art in Philadelphia and now lives in New York City. She illustrated the *Girl Scout Junior Handbook*.